Children praying.
NIGERIA

A Buddhist novice meditates in a monastery. BURMA

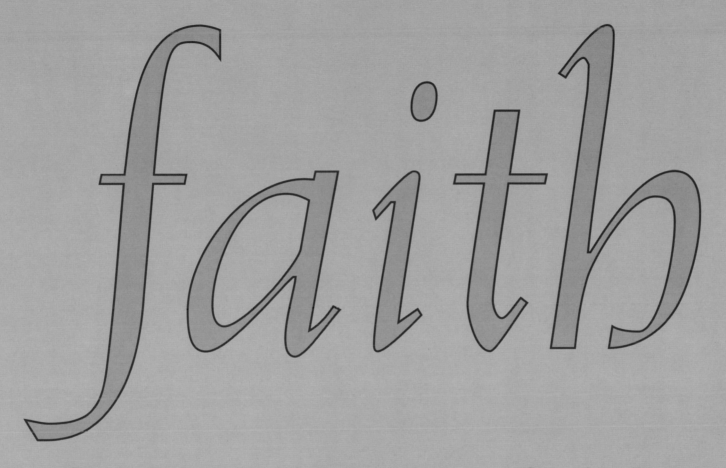

faith

Maya Ajmera ❖ Magda Nakassis ❖ Cynthia Pon

A GLOBAL FUND FOR
Children
BOOK

Charlesbridge

In our world,

Rastafarian. SOUTH AFRICA

Buddhist. CHINA (TIBET)

Christian. UNITED STATES

Jewish. UNITED STATES

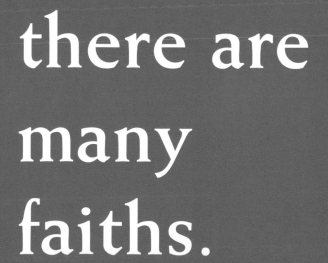

Daoist. CHINA
(HONG KONG)

Muslim. SAUDI ARABIA

there are
many
faiths.

Hindu. SRI LANKA

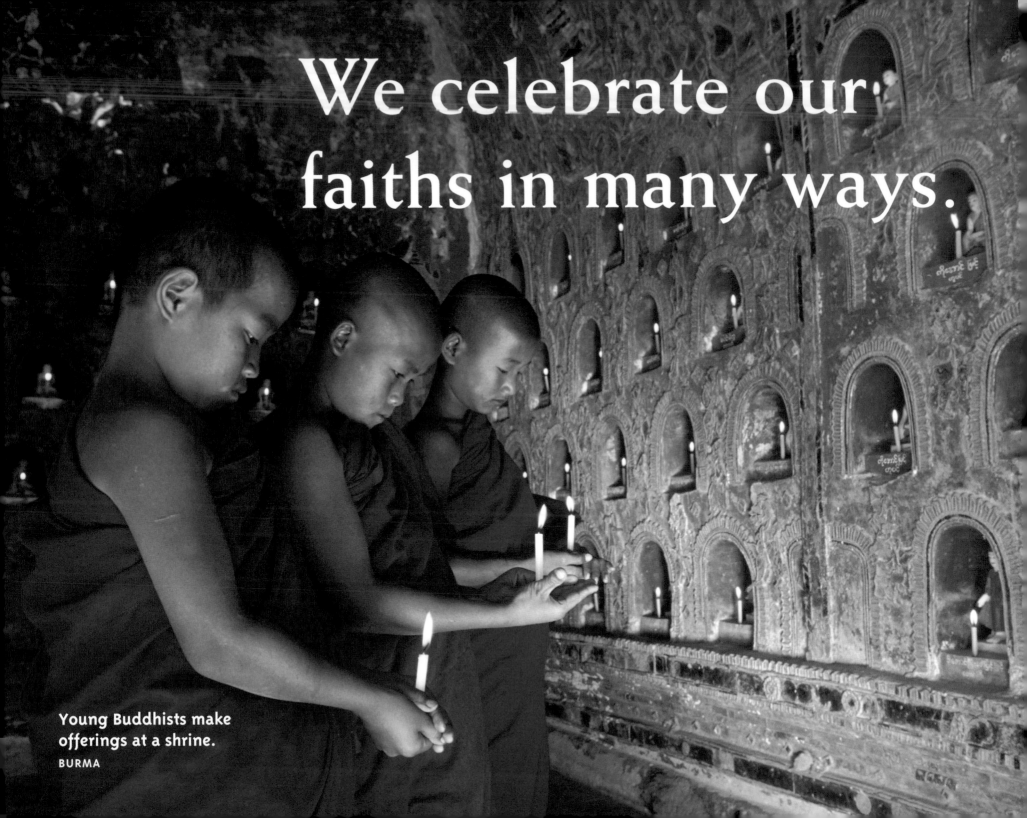

We celebrate our faiths in many ways.

Young Buddhists make offerings at a shrine.
BURMA

We pray.

A Sikh child prays at her mother's side. UNITED KINGDOM

A Muslim girl kneels on a prayer mat facing Mecca. TURKEY

We chant and we sing.

A boy chants Torah verses.
UNITED KINGDOM

Children singing on Moulid al-Nabi, the birthday of the prophet Mohammed. LIBYA

Christians chanting together
at a Syrian Orthodox service.
TURKEY

Studying the Qur'an.
KENYA

Holding a rosary while reading the Bible.
UNITED KINGDOM

A young Buddhist reads sutras. MONGOLIA

Young Orthodox Jews study prayer books. ISRAEL

We read our holy books.

Students at a Christian
Sunday School enjoy a visit
from a Buddhist monk.
SRI LANKA

Children focus
on the words
of a priest.
UNITED STATES

Listening attentively
at a madrassa, or
Islamic religious
school. INDONESIA

A father teaches
his son to sound
the shofar at
solemn Jewish
feasts.
UNITED STATES

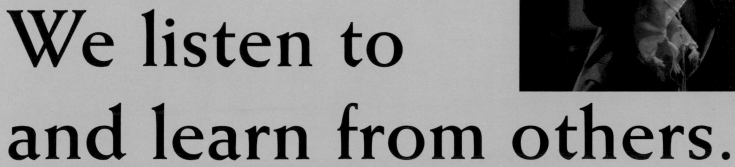

We listen to and learn from others.

We cleanse ourselves.

Performing a purifying
ritual using incense.
BOLIVIA

Baptizing a baby with holy water. NORWAY

A Hindu pilgrim bathes his child in the Ganges River. INDIA

Preparing for prayer at a mosque. BRUNEI

Paha Sapa, or
the Black Hills,
are sacred to
the Lakota
Indians.
UNITED STATES

A young girl lights candles in the
Church of the Holy Sepulchre.
ISRAEL

A girl visits a
mosque with her
brother. IRAQ

We visit holy places.

Gathering in front of the Bodhi tree, which is sacred to Buddhists. INDIA

We observe holidays in our homes or places of worship.

Children celebrate Night of the Dead (Noche de los Muertos). MEXICO

Father and son light a Hanukkah menorah. UNITED STATES

A girl celebrating Shichi-Go-San, or "Seven-Five-Three," a Shinto rite of passage, at a shrine. JAPAN

Making an offering at a Jain ritual. INDIA

Enjoying a Native American potlatch ceremony. UNITED STATES

Kids of different faiths celebrate Diwali with fireworks. INDIA

Celebrating Buddha's birthday. SOUTH KOREA

We celebrate with festivals.

Peeking out from under an Easter mask. GUATEMALA

Acting out the story of creation during the Apache Sunrise Ceremony.
UNITED STATES

Parsi children take part in Navjote, the Zoroastrian ritual of initiation. INDIA

Getting a first haircut at age three is an important tradition for some Jewish boys. ISRAEL

We mark the important events in our lives.

Ready to celebrate her First Holy Communion. MAURITIUS

Muslim girls in decorative head scarves. TURKEY

A Mennonite boy dressed in "plain clothes." UNITED STATES

A Hindu boy wearing a songket udeng, a ceremonial headdress. INDONESIA

We show our faiths through what we wear . . .

A Buddhist girl with thanaka face paint. BURMA

A boy wears a Patka, the traditional Sikh headdress for boys. UNITED KINGDOM

Jain girls show off their fancy headdresses before a procession. INDIA

and through what we eat and drink.

A grandfather teaches his granddaughter how to braid challah bread for the Jewish Sabbath meal. UNITED STATES

Receiving Holy Communion from a priest. UNITED STATES

A Muslim family at Iftar, breaking the daily fast during Ramadan. UNITED KINGDOM

We care for those around us

Bahá'í children share in the work and harvest of this community garden. MONGOLIA

Honoring a loved one at a funeral. ISRAEL

Showing respect to the spirit of a seal in the Shaman tradition.
RUSSIAN FEDERATION

and the lives that have sustained us.

A Muslim girl and her Christian best friend share a home at Concern for the Future, which serves displaced orphans. UGANDA

We respect others, making friends

Kids of different faiths share laughter and friendship. SRI LANKA

Native American pipe carriers in traditional dress. UNITED STATES

and building peace.

A Buddhist monk collects alms. BURMA

Kids volunteer with Habitat for Humanity
to build homes for others. UNITED STATES

We give to others,

A marabout, or Islamic spiritual
leader, receives a gift of food. MALI

and we help those in need.

Muslim. INDONESIA

Hindu. UNITED KINGDOM

Native religion. BRAZIL

Buddhist. CAMBODIA

Muslim. GAMBIA

Christian. AMERICAN SAMOA

Most of all, we hope.

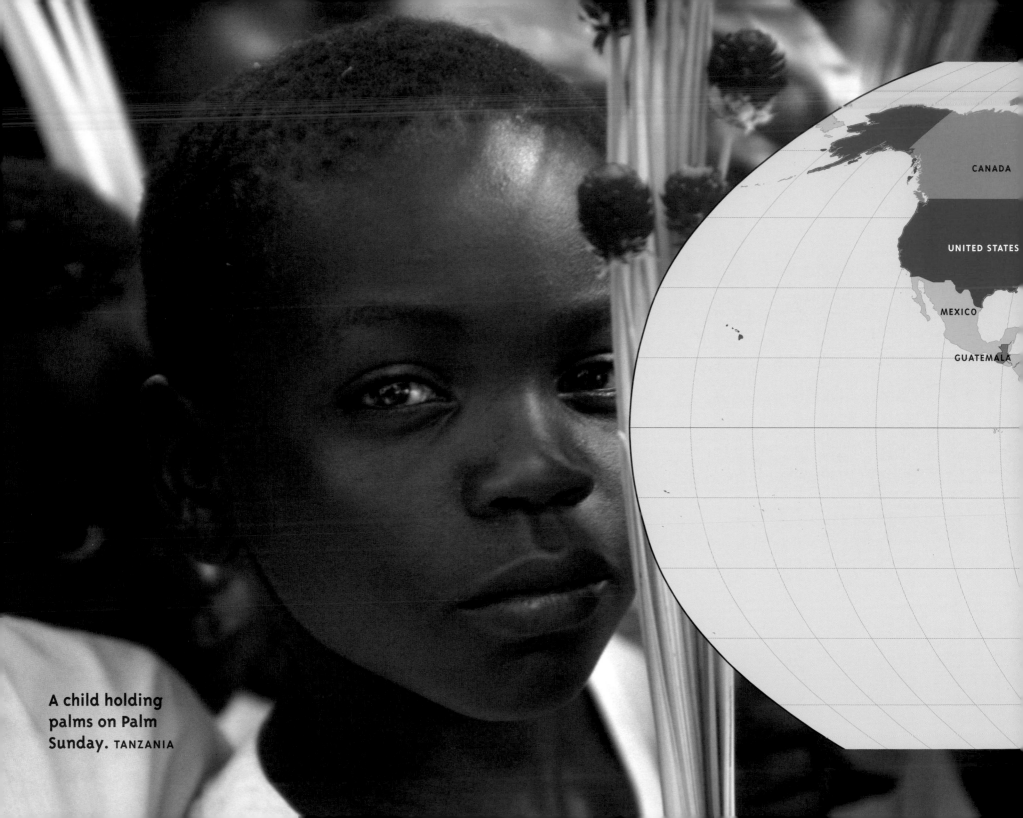

A child holding
palms on Palm
Sunday. TANZANIA

CANADA

UNITED STATES

MEXICO

GUATEMALA

This book features children from the places labeled on this map.

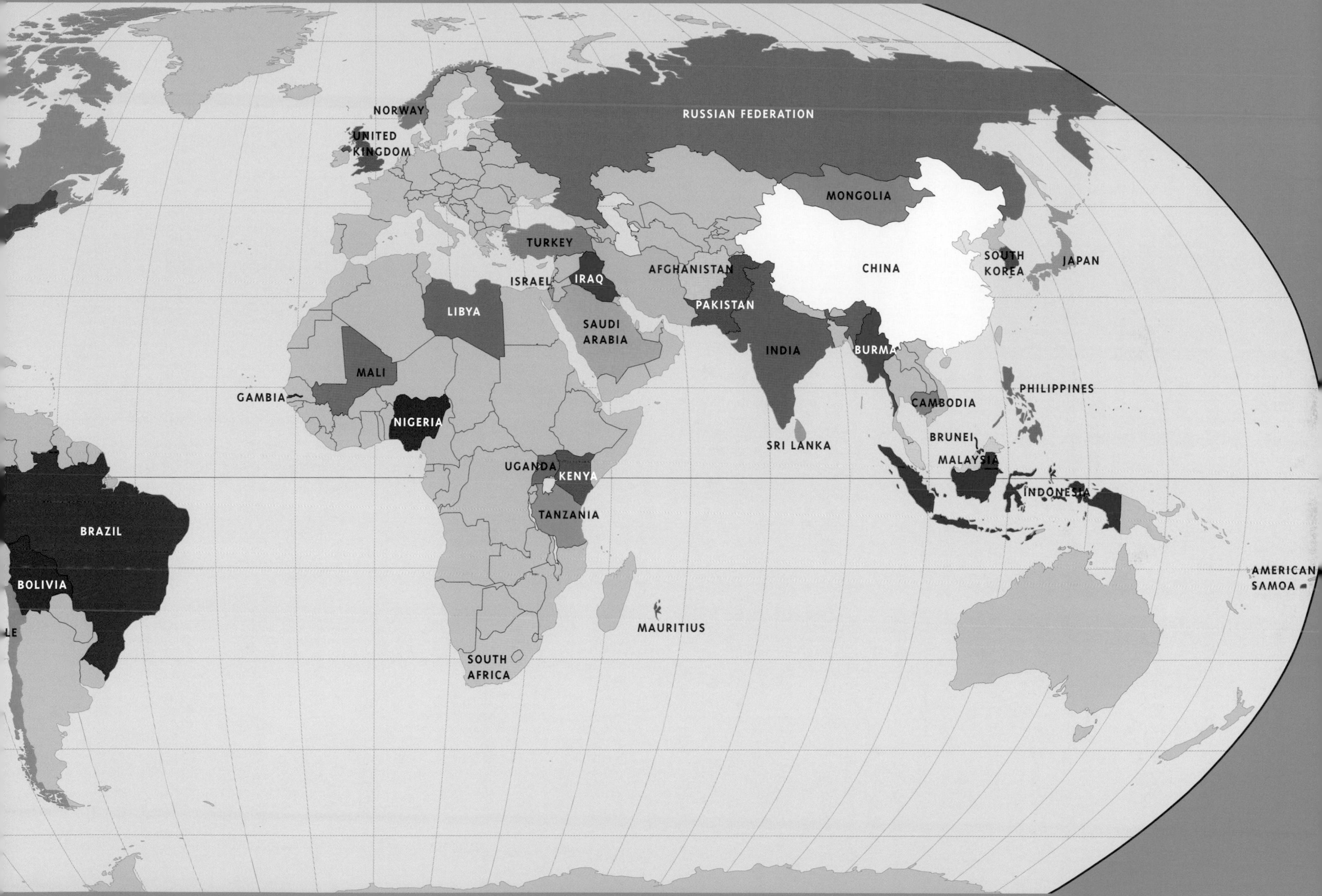

NORWAY

UNITED
KINGDOM

RUSSIAN FEDERATION

MONGOLIA

TURKEY

AFGHANISTAN

CHINA

SOUTH
KOREA

JAPAN

ISRAEL

IRAQ

LIBYA

PAKISTAN

SAUDI
ARABIA

INDIA

BURMA

MALI

PHILIPPINES

GAMBIA

CAMBODIA

NIGERIA

UGANDA

SRI LANKA

BRUNEI

KENYA

MALAYSIA

TANZANIA

INDONESIA

BRAZIL

MAURITIUS

AMERICAN
SAMOA

BOLIVIA

LE

SOUTH
AFRICA

Elements of Faith

Aymara Indian children in front of a church in the Andes mountains. CHILE

Praying

When people pray, they talk with someone or something greater than themselves. It may not be something they can see or touch, but they know it is important to them. Sometimes people pray for help or comfort. Sometimes they pray to give thanks or praise. They pray alone and with others. A prayer can be formal words that people recite, or it can be something people create to express how they think and feel. Prayers may be made at different times: for example, at special events like weddings, at certain times of the day, or before a meal.

Sometimes it is clear when another person is praying: a Christian may make the sign of the cross, and a Muslim may face the holy city of Mecca. Others may dance or chant. Still others may keep silent. Instead of praying, followers of some Eastern traditions, such as Buddhism, Hinduism, and Daoism, may meditate by being still and listening to the world in a deeper way. Praying and meditating are just two ways of practicing a faith, but they are a big part of many spiritual traditions around the world.

Chanting and Singing

People often sing or chant prayers and hymns out loud. Chanting is a rhythmic way of speaking. People may chant and sing when they are alone, in front of a gathering of faithful people, or as part of a group, such as a church choir. Members of many different faiths, such as the Tuvan throat singers of central Asia, chant their names for God or repeat sounds that call upon the spirits or ancestors. Singing can help bring a community together, as members' voices join as one. It can be a fun and energetic way to celebrate faith.

Reading Holy Books

Holy books help many children around the world learn how to read and write, as well as learn about their religion. Sometimes holy books are called scriptures or texts. Many of the stories in these books come from an oral tradition. They were passed down from person to person, but have since

been written down. The oldest holy books are thousands of years old. They contain stories about creation and divine acts, lessons on how to live a good life, prayers, laws, and sometimes prophecies, or predictions about the future. Many people first read these rich and fascinating books as children but continue to study them for a lifetime.

Listening and Learning

Listening to others is another way people can learn about faith. Often people look to older members of their community for wisdom and advice. Many children go to religious schools—some every day, and others just on their day of rest, or what some faiths refer to as the Sabbath. Children who grow up in interfaith families may celebrate from an early age the beliefs and rituals of more than one faith.

Cleansing

Cleaning the body is often a symbol for cleansing the soul, or the spiritual part of a person. It is a way for people to make themselves pure and keep away harmful thoughts, feelings, and actions. It can also be a way to celebrate an important event, join a community, or prepare to enter a holy place. Many cleansing ceremonies involve water. The water may come from a sacred, or holy, place, or it may be blessed by a religious leader. In some faiths cleansing takes place through fire and smoke. Cleansing oneself is a physical way to connect the body and the soul.

Holy Places

There are many different kinds of holy places. A holy place can be as small as a room or as large as a city. Many holy places are houses of worship, such as temples or mosques, that are built specifically for a religious community. But a holy place does not have to have four walls. It can be a mountain, a tree, a shrine on the street, or any place that makes people feel connected to their faith. Sometimes people known as pilgrims go on special trips, or pilgrimages, to holy places to pray or to meet other members of their religious community. Holy places can inspire wonder and awe. They are places where people feel safe and where they can learn to make peace with themselves and others.

Indigenous children in a Muslim village. PAKISTAN

Holidays and Festivals

Holiday comes from the words *holy* and *day*, and originally meant a day set aside by a religious group to honor sacred events or people. Some holidays are now enjoyed by entire cultures or countries, not just by members of a certain faith. On religious holidays people celebrate their faiths, their families, and their communities. Often they wear distinctive clothing, eat special foods, attend religious services, or perform certain acts, such as giving to the poor. Holidays are a time to take a break from the routines of school or work and to give thanks and honor what is good. Festivals, like holidays, can be religious celebrations, but they often last more than one day and tend to be held in public places, such as city streets. Festivals are a time of great joy, when people sing, dance, pray, get dressed up, have parades, and have fun.

Marking Important Events

Most faiths mark certain events in a child's life with special rituals or celebrations. Many of these events, such as the Zoroastrian Navjote ritual, a Jewish bar or bat mitzvah, or the rite of First Communion in some Christian traditions, center around growing up and becoming a full member of a faith community. Children celebrate these occasions with their families and often with their larger communities. Many of these ceremonies have existed for centuries, and their traditions are passed on from generation to generation.

Dress

The clothes and jewelry that a person wears can be a way to identify his or her faith. Members of many religions tend to keep their heads, faces, or bodies covered with special garments, such as yarmulkes or hijabs. The way people dress can also tell others about their roles within their religious communities. The style of turban that a Sikh boy wears, for example, changes as he gets older. A Muslim may dress in two long white sheets on his pilgrimage to Mecca. On special occasions, both children and adults in many faiths may dress up and wear distinctive clothes. These can range from a formal suit for a funeral to a fancy or playful outfit for a festival.

Children pray during a Buddhist ceremony for victims of the 2004 tsunami. SRI LANKA

Ramadan, not eating from sunrise to sunset. Trying some of the special foods of a different religious culture can be an appetizing way to learn about another faith.

Caring for and Helping Others

Service to others is a part of every faith. People care for others by celebrating happy occasions, such as weddings or births, and helping others through difficult times, such as illnesses or the deaths of loved ones. Serving others also means giving to and helping those in need, including those outside one's own community. This can be done by adding a few coins to the collection plate at a place of worship, sharing food with someone who is hungry, donating to a charity, or speaking up when another has been wronged. Taking care of the broader community, including animals and the environment, is an important part of many faiths.

Food and Drink

What people eat and drink is a big part of their culture and often an important part of their faith. Special foods are part of many religious occasions. At other times, people avoid eating certain foods to show their spiritual devotion. Some faiths have rules about food and drink that believers follow all the time. For example, strict Hindus never eat beef, and some Jews follow rules called kashrut that are explained in their holy books. Other faiths have rules for people to follow at certain times. Some Christians do not eat meat on Fridays, and Muslims fast during the month of

The world has many faiths and many different sets of beliefs and practices. Respecting and working to understand the differences among faiths helps create a more peaceful and just society. Making friends with people from different religious backgrounds can be a rewarding and fun first step in learning about other faiths.

Words to Know

A girl shaking the lulav (a palm branch) during Sukkot, the Jewish harvest festival. CANADA

alms: money, goods, or food given as charity to the poor or to support members of religious communities.

altar: a raised table or platform used as a center of religious worship and ritual.

ancestor: a relative from whom one is descended.

Bahá'í Faith: a faith whose purpose is to unite all races and peoples in one global society and one common faith. Bahá'ís are the followers of Bahá'u'lláh (meaning "Glory of God"), who they believe is the most recent in a line of Divine Messengers.

baptism: the rite by which a person becomes a Christian by immersing in water or having water sprinkled on his or her head, so as to begin a new life in Jesus Christ.

bar mitzvah or bat mitzvah: an initiation ceremony for Jewish boys (bar mitzvah) and girls (bat mitzvah), held when they formally join their congregations, usually around age thirteen. It celebrates their passage into adulthood and their readiness to take on religious responsibilities.

Muslim boy with prayer rug during Friday prayers. MALAYSIA

Buddhism: a faith whose followers seek to end suffering by living according to the teachings of Siddhartha Gautama, or the Buddha (meaning "one who is awake").

Christianity: a faith whose followers celebrate the life and teachings of Jesus Christ (Christ means "the anointed one"). They believe Jesus is the Son of God sent to Earth to teach people about God's love and the forgiveness of sins.

church: a place used for public worship, usually of the Christian faith.

community: a group of people who have something in common, such as their faith.

Confucianism: a set of moral teachings passed down by Confucius and his students in ancient China. Followers believe that benevolence (humaneness to one another) is the highest virtue.

Daoism: a religion and philosophy that began in China. Dao means "path" or "way." Followers believe in the unity of all and emphasize simplicity, playfulness, and harmony with the universe.

dervish: a member of one of several Muslim religious groups, some of whom perform whirling dances while praying.

Diwali: a holiday celebrated most commonly by Hindus, Jains, and Sikhs around the world. Also known as the Festival of Light, Diwali celebrates the triumph of good over evil and often features fireworks, festive clothing, and food.

divine: something from, or related to, a god or goddess.

Easter: the most important Christian feast, celebrating the resurrection, or return to life, of Christ after his death on the cross as an act of freeing people from the slavery of sin.

Hanukkah: an eight-day-long Jewish holiday, also called the Festival of Lights, that celebrates the rededication of the Temple of Jerusalem after a victory over invaders. Many families light a special candleholder called a menorah during this holiday.

hijab: a head scarf, often with a veil, worn by some Muslim girls and women.

Hinduism: a faith whose followers, called Hindus, believe that God or the divine can take many forms. Through worship of a chosen deity, Hindus seek to be reborn in higher

forms until the soul is finally united with the divine.

Holi: a popular and lively Hindu spring festival. Also called the Festival of Colors, Holi is often celebrated in India by followers of other religions as well.

Holy Communion: a ritual recalling Jesus' last meal with his friends, in which believers eat bread and wine that represent the body and blood of Christ. For many people this creates a union with Christ.

Whirling dervish. TURKEY

Hindu children. INDONESIA

incense: a substance frequently burned as part of a religious ritual, typically for purification. Incense usually has a strong, sweet smell.

Islam: a faith whose followers are called Muslims and who submit themselves to the will of Allah, which is Arabic for "God." Muslims believe Allah revealed His words to the Prophet Mohammed, and these revelations make up the religion's holy book, the Qur'an.

Jainism: a faith that began in India whose followers have a strong respect for life, practice nonviolence, and believe they must not harm any living thing.

Judaism: a faith whose followers worship one God and follow the laws of the Torah. Followers believe in a special relationship, or covenant, between God and Abraham that extends to his descendants.

meditation: a spiritual practice by which one keeps the mind clear and open, breathes slowly, and listens to the world in a deeper way.

monastery: a peaceful place where a community of religious men or women live and study their religion.

mosque: a Muslim house of worship.

native religions: There are many native religions, also called indigenous or folk religions, around the world.

Many share close ties to the natural world, a belief in the supernatural, special rituals and traditions, and an understanding that faith is an inseparable part of each person.

Navjote: an initiation ritual through which a child becomes a full member of the Zoroastrian religion. For the ceremony a child wears a sacred shirt, symbolizing purity and renewal, and a sacred thread, symbolizing universal fellowship, is wrapped around his or her waist.

pilgrimage: a journey to a shrine or other sacred place. One who goes on a pilgrimage is called a pilgrim.

Ramadan: a month of daytime fasting for Muslims as a way to purify oneself and to learn compassion and self-control. The feast of Eid al-Fitr celebrates the end of Ramadan.

Easter Vigil. UNITED STATES

Rastafarianism: a faith whose followers revere Haile Selassie, the last emperor of Ethiopia, and believe he was a messenger sent from God to teach them how to live. Most members are of Afro-Caribbean origin and wear their hair in dreadlocks.

ritual: a ceremony or a formal set of words or actions significant to a certain religion.

rosary: a string of beads used as a counting aid for repetitive prayer.

Sabbath: a specific day of the week set aside by a faith for rest and worship. The Sabbath is generally Friday for Muslims, Saturday for Jews, and Sunday for Christians.

sacred: something holy or important to members of a faith.

scriptures: a book or a set of writings, such as the Christian Bible, the Hebrew Torah, or the Muslim Qur'an, that is holy to followers of a religion. Hindus regard the Vedas as one of their sacred texts. Buddhists have many sacred texts, which they call sutras. The revered texts for Confucianism, the Bahá'í Faith, and Shintoism are, respectively, the Five Classics, the Kitáb-i-Aqdas, and the Kojiki.

Shamanism: a faith in which a person called a shaman communicates with and influences the spirit world, often for the purpose of healing sickness or controlling supernatural forces.

A Native American pipe dancer. UNITED STATES

Bathing in holy waters. PHILIPPINES

Shintoism: a faith practiced in Japan whose followers worship many gods and believe in the power of kami (spirits). Followers have a strong respect for their elders, families, communities, and traditions.

shofar: a ram's horn trumpet blown on occasions sacred to the Jewish religion, including the holidays Rosh Hashanah and Yom Kippur.

shrine: a sacred place, building, or case that contains a sacred object.

Sikhism: a faith whose followers believe in one God and practice constant devotion to God. Sikhs believe that everyone is equal in God's eyes. The Sikh scriptures, the Guru Granth Sahib, serve as a guru, or teacher, to help followers build a personal relationship with God.

soul: according to some faiths, the inner self that makes people who they are. Some people believe that the soul lives on after the body dies. Soul and spirit can sometimes mean the same thing.

spirit: according to many faiths, a part of each person that is separate from the body and that gives the body life. Other faiths believe that spirits are supernatural and exist both within a person and outside the body.

spiritual: related to something sacred, holy, or religious.

synagogue: a Jewish house of worship.

temple: a house of worship in many faiths.

turban: a headdress worn by some Sikhs, many male Muslims, and some members of other religions and cultures.

worship: to pray, respect, and deeply love a god, goddess, or significant religious figure.

yarmulke: a skullcap most often worn by Jewish boys and men.

Zoroastrianism: a faith whose followers worship the god Ahura Mazda and follow the teachings of the prophet Zoroaster. Some members of the community who were originally from Persia settled in India and became known as Parsis. Fire is held sacred as a sign of divine presence and the human ability to choose good over evil.

Photo Credits

Enjoying jalabi, an Afghan pastry, at the end of Ramadan.
AFGHANISTAN

To my grandparents for their faith and conviction—M. A.

For my Auntie Rose, who cannot help but give to and care for everyone who has the pleasure of knowing her—M. N.

Glory to God in the highest and on earth peace among people of God's grace—C. P.

Faith was developed by The Global Fund for Children (www.globalfundforchildren.org), a nonprofit organization committed to advancing the dignity of children and youth around the world. Global Fund for Children Books teach young people to value diversity and help them become productive and caring citizens of the world.

Text copyright © 2009 by Maya Ajmera, Magda Nakassis, and Cynthia Pon
Photographs copyright © by individual copyright holders

Developed by The Global Fund for Children
1101 Fourteenth Street NW, Suite 420
Washington, DC 20005
(202) 331-9003
www.globalfundforchildren.org

Published by Charlesbridge, 85 Main Street, Watertown, MA 02472 (617) 926-0329
www.charlesbridge.com

Part of the proceeds from this book's sales will be donated to The Global Fund for Children to support innovative community-based organizations that serve the world's most vulnerable children and youth. Details about the donation of royalties can be obtained by writing to Charlesbridge Publishing and The Global Fund for Children.

Library of Congress Cataloging-in-Publication Data
Ajmera, Maya.
    Faith / Maya Ajmera, Magda Nakassis, and Cynthia Pon.
        p. cm.
    ISBN 978-1-58089-177-6 (reinforced for library use)
    ISBN 978-1-58089-178-3 (softcover)
1. Religion—Juvenile literature. 2. Religions—Juvenile literature.
I. Nakassis, Magda. II. Pon, Cynthia. III. Title.
BL48.A36 2009
200—dc22   2008008282

Printed in China
(hc) 10 9 8 7 6 5 4 3 2 1
(sc) 10 9 8 7 6 5 4 3 2 1

Display type and text type set in Weiss; caption type set in TriplexBold
Color separations by Chroma Graphics, Singapore
Printed and bound by Regent Publishing Services
Production supervision by Brian G. Walker
Designed by Susan Mallory Sherman

Acknowledgments

We thank the following friends and readers who responded to our queries about the many faiths and their cultural contexts and interrelations covered in this project. *Faith* has been enriched by their gracious and generous feedback.

John Beeching (Maryknoll Brother), Chris Byrnes (Harvard Divinity School), Francisca Cho (Georgetown University), John Cort (Denison University), Sonia Dhami (The Sikh Foundation), Paramjit Singh Dhillon (Guru Gobind Singh Children's Foundation), Rabbi Yosef Edelstein, John Esposito (Georgetown University), John Kartje (Archdiocese of Chicago), Kathryn Lohre (The Pluralism Project, Harvard University), Tom Michel (Society of Jesus), Deonnie Moodie (The Pluralism Project, Harvard University), Ellen Price (Office of Media and Public Information, United States Bahá'í National Center), Stephen Prothero (Boston University), Buffy Sainte-Marie (The Nihewan Foundation), Rabbi Zvi Teitelbaum, and Aaron Weintraub (The Sixth & I Historic Synagogue, Washington DC). Thanks to Kelly Swanson Turner for help in the research and development of this book.